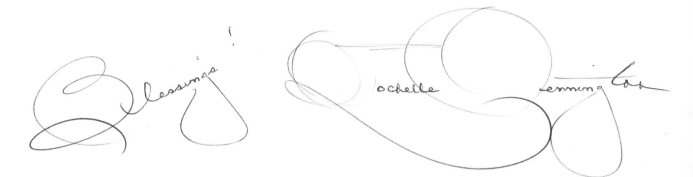

Blessings!

ochelle ennington

The Christmas Tree Ship

Published by
The Guest Cottage, Inc.
dba Amherst Press
8821 Hwy 47
Woodruff, Wisconsin 54568
www.theguestcottage.com

The Clipper Ship Gallery
10 W. Harris Avenue
La Grange, IL 60525
http://www.charlesvickery.com

For information on this and other books from The Guest Cottage, call 800-333-8122.

ISBN#1-930596-19-7

The Christmas Tree Ship

The Story of Captain Santa

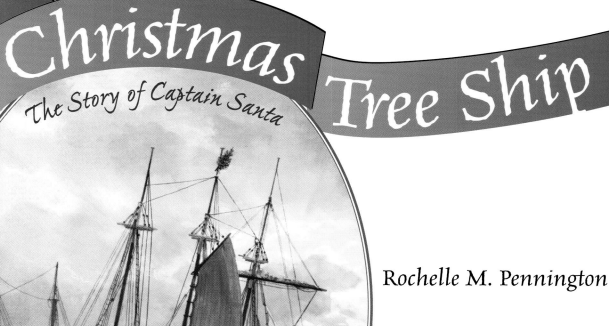

Rochelle M. Pennington

featuring the Art
of Charles Vickery

The
Guest
Cottage, Inc.
dba Amherst Press

Woodruff, Wisconsin

First and foremost, I would like to thank my publisher, Nancy Ravanelli, and her extraordinary staff at The Guest Cottage. Their dedication and tireless efforts on behalf of *The Christmas Tree Ship* were amazing.

Special thanks to The Jacobs Family at The Clipper Ship Gallery for extending permission to use Charles Vickery's beautiful artwork. An invaluable contribution!

Deepest gratitude to H. Jackson Brown, "my old buddy in Nashville," for his endorsement, friendship and guidance over the past many years. He has blessed me more than he will ever know. And to Mrs. Rosemary Brown, sincere thanks for faithful prayers over my life.

Heartfelt appreciation to Jack Canfield for the generosity of his endorsement and to his entire staff at the *Chicken Soup for the Soul* office. Everyone there is so special, as special as their hope to change the world. Please know this: you have changed *my* world. Your books have been, and continue to be, a wellspring of inspiration to me.

Endless thanks to the many research specialists who provided historical material from archives at the following institutes: Chicago Historical Society, Wisconsin Maritime Museum, Rogers Street Fishing Village Museum, Milwaukee Public Library Marine Room and the Great Lakes Center for Archival Collections at Bowling Green State University. Special thanks to Southport Video for providing underwater footage of the shipwreck site.

Much gratitude to Lee Murdock and Carl Behrend, both singer/songwriters in the Great Lakes region who have recorded ballads about the legend. It was a privilege working with each of you.

Sincere appreciation to Gloria Hansen at The Cupola House in Door County, WI whose support through the whole process was such a blessing!

Special thanks to sweet Maggie Becker for sharing her captain's wheel with me and to my best friend in the whole wide world, Linda Vis, for helping with costumes. To Kurt Moore for graciously allowing use of his pier and to all "my people" at E P Direct for assistance with the sketches, thanks so much!

Deepest gratitude to my dear folks and to all my brothers and sisters whose steadfast encouragement means the world to me! A very special thank you to my brother-in-law, David Roehrig, and to my mother, Gloria Serwe, for posing for the sketches.

Ultimately, my most heartfelt acknowledgment belongs, of course, to my husband and children, to whom this book is dedicated. Their love makes everything I do possible. Thank you for believing in my dreams and believing in me.

Dedicated to the loves of my life,
Leslie, Nicholas and Erica

The year was 1912. The month, November. Autumn had fallen asleep in Northern Michigan, and Winter was just rising. It was rising on the land first, then heading into the waters, closing them up, freezing them solid for a while. Not yet, but shortly. There was still time for Captain Schuenemann to make his last sail of the season—a little time, but not much. He needed to hurry if he didn't want to meet Old Man Winter out on the waters, the worst possible place. He knew this, and was doing just that— hurrying, hurrying. The winds were telling him, and the waves also, "Hurry, Captain, hurry." Whispering, whispering were these voices around him in those moments at the break of dawn. He listened.

Then the captain reached a decision: "We sail." He would delay no further. Thick ropes anchoring the wooden ship to the shore began to be untied.

Captain Schuenemann was on his way to Chicago with a load of fresh Christmas trees, a majestic cargo of Yuletide cheer. Five thousand evergreens filled the ship's belly, with another five hundred tied to its decks. Pine scented the harbor and those gathered there breathed in deeply this first fragrance of Christmas.

The last tree brought aboard, a spruce, was then fastened to the tip of the top of the tallest of three sails, as was the particular tradition of this particular ship. From here, this place of honor, it adorned both the vessel and its holiday load, like a star atop a tree, but instead, a tree atop a ship, a crown of sorts, the identifying mark of *The Christmas Tree Ship.*

Every Christmas, the captain and his sailing vessel made this voyage, together, down to the Clark Street Bridge in Chicago, just off Michigan Avenue. Captain Schuenemann waited the whole long year for this very journey, his favorite of all. He loved Christmas, and loved delivering his trees to the docks, as he had done since 1887, where he sold them right off his ship for as little as a quarter or as much as a whole dollar. And what a sight his ship was with wreaths hung from every rail!

To the folks in Chicago who awaited its annual arrival, the ship had become a symbol of Christmas itself, and its blue-eyed captain, a hero. His generosity in giving free Christmas trees away to churches, orphanages, and to any family who otherwise wouldn't have been able to afford one, gave cause for him to acquire a nickname: Captain Santa. Hearing it made the ruddy-faced skipper smile, especially when spoken by the children. They'd be waiting for him on the docks when he approached the harbor, edging his ship in, shores parting before it. "Captain Santa's here! Captain Santa!" they'd shout.

Soon he'd hear their voices again, and then soon he'd be back home. This is what he told his wife of these many years as she stood there on the pier beside him. She wanted to know about the ship's return, and his also. She always did. When the waters separated them, her heart from his, his from hers, she wondered when he would be home. And he would tell her the same answer each time he left, "Soon. I'll be home soon." It was an unchanging response to her unchanging question. Yet still she asked, and still he answered.

Then dawn broke forth into day on that November morning, lingering for just a moment in shades of violet, crimson and gold. Lingering, this dawn, like the captain's dear wife on the planks of a paintless pier where she waved goodbye, waving with the waters, "Goodbye, Captain, goodbye."

The great ship was set in motion, this 44-year-old aging schooner, weathered and weary, in the twilight of its sailing days. With Chicago somewhere before them, and Thompson's Landing in the Upper Peninsula of Michigan now behind, the captain's hands grabbed hold of the wooden wheel with its spokes and spines that would navigate his vessel through unseen passageways in the open waters spreading themselves before him.

To his crew waiting on deck, Captain Schuenemann called out, "Unleash the sails! Raise 'em high!" And so they did.

Oh, to know what comes alive in the heart of a sailor at such a moment as this, to experience the exhilaration of it all!

Then the captain saw it. It was the one sight he loved more than any other when he was out to sea, this very sight, the sight of seemingly being able to see forever across endless waters and an endless horizon.

Somewhere out there Chicago lay. The captain knew it. But for now, it appeared not to be so. For now, it looked as if he and his ship, with its sails raised high, could sail on forever into infinity. He embraced the sight with his arms spread wide across the width of the wheel he worked before him. *Sail on, Captain, sail on.*

Yes, if there was a sight more beautiful than this, the captain knew not what it was. And he had seen many—especially out here where moonbeams gathered at midnight to dance on a watery floor beneath lanterns hung high in the sky. And he would dance with them, this captain, shuffling his feet on the deck to music he alone could hear—gulls singing lullabies on the shore and foghorns calling out in deep-throated voices.

Then slumber would beckon to him, and he would sleep in Life's arms as it rocked him, back and forth, back and forth. In the great rocking chair of the waters, the captain would be rocked to a rhythm of heartbeats, the water's and his own. Tide in, tide out. Breath in, breath out. *Sleep now, Captain, sleep.*

But on that November 23rd morning of 1912, sleep was the furthest thing from the captain's mind. He was awake, wide-eyed awake, acutely aware of the signs around him.

From where he stood at the helm of his ship, he turned around, again and again, looking over his shoulder, watching the gray sky behind him darken. This was no passing glance he gave the sky and its warning, but a fixed stare, worry creasing itself deeply into his brow. This changing sky meant something, and the changing current that pulled itself around him did, too. They were silent sirens telling him, "Run, Captain, run." Winter had awoken, and it was coming for him.

Winds were rising higher and higher, temperatures were falling lower and lower, and forty foot waves were crashing over breaker walls along shorelines just past. Ahead of these heavy seas, Captain Schuenemann was running, his only choice. He couldn't turn back, it was too late for that. His ship was already taking on snow and ice from the blizzard that was wrapping itself around it. Winter was chasing him down in the most ferocious of ways, closing in on him in the form of a mid-lateral cyclone. This was the term weathermen later used to explain what happened out there on the waters when the sky turned black and the world turned white, and Winter caught the captain.

The Rouse Simmons at dockside in Chicago, 1910.
Courtesy of Chicago Historical Society

1910 photo of U.S. Lifesaving Station crew members at Two Rivers believed to be the same crew involved in the 1912 rescue attempts of the Rouse Simmons. Courtesy of Rogers Street Fishing Village Museum.

A crew of rescue workers on duty at the United States Lifesaving Station (a predecessor organization of the Coast Guard) in Kewaunee, Wisconsin, picked up the captain's distress signals and radioed south to the Two Rivers station where a crew headed into the storm to help the ship, coming close enough— within an eighth of a mile—to catch sight of the battered vessel coated in ice, and iced in snow. Then a blinding squall of white passed between the two, eliminating all visibility with its heavy curtain of snow. When it passed, *The Christmas Tree Ship* had vanished.

Yes, those brave rescue workers almost made it, but Winter made it first, bearing down upon the loaded ship with the full force of its weight. *The Christmas Tree Ship* could no longer sustain itself above the waters, and so, with the weight of a single snowflake more, it sunk below.

Two weeks and six days later, fishermen came across a corked bottle floating in waters near Sheboygan, Wisconsin.

Within, on a torn sheet of paper ripped from Captain Schuenemann's own log, was written his farewell address: "Everybody, goodbye. I guess we are thru. Leaking badly. God help us. Signed: Herman Schuenemann."

Newspapers broke the story, including the headline printed in the Friday, December 13, 1912 issue of the Chicago American: *Lost Ship's Story Told in a Bottle.*

It had taken two weeks and six days to find the bottle, but for the ship itself, it would take another fifty-eight years. A scuba diver came across the wreckage quite by accident while searching for another sunken vessel off the coast of Two Rivers, Wisconsin, in 1971. There she was, *The Christmas Tree Ship*, intact and sitting upright on the bottom of Lake Michigan. He recognized the legendary ship immediately, its trees still fastened to its deck, secured there, just as they had been that fateful day long ago, preserved in the frigid waters. This unshovelled grave of the captain had been marked by a tree, as if a grave upon the land, marked by a spruce, fastened to the tip of the top of the tallest of three sails way back when.

1884 photograph of the Rouse Simmons
(Courtesy of Wisconsin Maritime Museum)

And so it was, that such a tree as this was fastened to a sail on another old, wooden ship being loaded with evergreens the following November of 1913 at Thompson's Landing. This voyage had been chartered by a woman of remarkable courage who stood on the planks of the same paintless pier where she had stood a year earlier, almost to the very day. Her name was Barbara, the captain's beloved wife, and under her eye, evergreens were going aboard this ship until it was time for her to begin her journey. And then she did.

Stepping off the pier and onto this vessel named *Fearless*, she and her precious cargo of white pine and balsam and fir were bound for Chicago where the city was waiting. They had heard, you see, that Mrs. Santa was on her way.

When her schooner sailed in, the people of Chicago were gathered on the docks just off of Michigan Avenue to welcome the Captain's darling. They came by carriage and they came by sleigh and they came on foot, whole families hand-in-hand, to buy an evergreen from this noble woman who chose to stand in the gap between the past and the present and become heir to the tradition that was a part of their holiday and a part of their hearts.

For the next twenty-one years, Mrs. Herman Schuenemann set sail in November to honor her husband's memory and his love of the Christ of Christmas, the everlasting hope he held fast to for all of his days like a great wheel navigating him onward.

Somewhere out there, heaven lay. The captain knew it, for the horizon had shown him it was so through the one sight he loved more than any other when he was out to sea. This hope of life eternal, of life evermore, guided his heart. It was his soul's compass, its beacon, its North Star.

"I'll be home soon," the captain told his dear Barbara when they waved goodbye to one another for the last time.

And so he was. It just hadn't been clear to which home he would be returning that day. It would be the eternal one that unfolded itself around him in those moments when his ship went down and his soul went up, and he was carried by his hope to A Place More Beautiful.

Here, beyond the horizon, from the ship of his soul, the captain sails through the unseen passageways of eternity and looks upon forever, and ever and ever.

Sail on, Captain, sail on.

Artist Charles Vickery's dramatic paintings earned him recognition as one of the finest seascape artists of our time. Best known for his renditions of the sea, its coastlines, ports and majestic sailing vessels, what most captivates viewers is the way he could capture the infinite moods of water. His paintings come to life in a style defined by the artist as "realism with a dash of romance."

For more information about Mr. Vickery's original paintings and fine art limited edition reproductions, please contact:

The Clipper Ship Gallery
10 W. Harris Avenue
La Grange, IL 60525
1-800-750-7327

Or visit the gallery's website at:
www.charlesvickery.com